Rutland

IN OLD PHOTOGRAPHS

Rutland's rural idyll: a thatched cottage and rustic garden at Wing, photographed by G.M. Henton in 1915.

Rutland

IN OLD PHOTOGRAPHS

Compiled by TIM CLOUGH

ALAN
SUTTON

Alan Sutton Publishing Limited
Phoenix Mill · Far Thrupp
Stroud · Gloucestershire

in association with Leicestershire Museums,
Arts & Records Service

First published 1993

Copyright © T.H.McK. Clough and
Leicestershire Museums, Arts & Records
Service

British Library Cataloguing in Publication Data

A catalogue record for this book is available
from the British Library

ISBN 0 86299 528 0

Typeset in 9/10 Sabon.
Typesetting and origination by
Alan Sutton Publishing Limited.
Printed in Great Britain by
Redwood Books, Trowbridge.

Contents

A crisp winter scene at Ayston in about 1905. A heavy hoar-frost adorns magnificent beech trees on the edge of the village – an ideal opportunity for the photographer.

Introduction

'What is the smallest county in England?' the quizmaster would ask. 'Rutland!' would come the reply – and until 1974 this was the correct answer. Since then, Rutland has been a district within Leicestershire, but it retains the same boundaries with only minor alterations, and remains very much on the map.

Within Rutland's historic borders there lies a stretch of countryside which, in its variety of town and village, is a microcosm of rural England. The lighter soils and limestones of its eastern parishes contrast with the warmer rust-red ironstones of central and southern Rutland, while the heavier, clayey soils of the western borderland with Leicestershire recall distant days when royal forest was a barrier. Medieval ridge-and-furrow fields can still be seen in some areas, while elsewhere the whole landscape has been taken apart for the extraction of iron ore and building stone and then reinstated. The Great North Road, a legacy of the Romans, bisects it on the east, while the Victorians overlaid Rutland with a web of railways. Nowhere was there a major industrial centre, but life centred on arable and dairy farming and all the trades that supplied the farmer's and householder's needs.

Small wonder that the oft-quoted phrase *'multum in parvo'* – meaning 'much in little' – was adopted as Rutland's motto, or indeed that the first photographers, in the mid-nineteenth century, found plenty to record. Our fortune is that during the succeeding century, and a half, while the world has been changing at a rate never before dreamed of, the camera has produced an irreplaceable archive of memorable images to record these changes.

Many of these photographs were taken by professional or serious amateur photographers. Foremost among them must be G.M. Henton, a Leicester photographer whose negatives are now in the Leicestershire Record Office. He made many visits to Rutland in the early years of the twentieth century, and a considerable number of his views are included. The identification of a motorcycle belonging to an Oakham photographer, Henry Ellingworth, in a view at Lyndon (page 151) raises the question of the extent to which these early photographers worked together. Ellingworth himself was typical of the high street retailer, selling photographic and artists' materials and more besides, who also took studio photographs, portraits and groups, and published postcards of newsworthy events. His nearest rivals included A.E. Billows of Oakham and W.J.W. Stocks of Uppingham, while at Hambleton the schoolmaster S. Cooke indulged in photography as a serious hobby and produced some extremely good pictures.

The Rutland County Museum possesses two significant groups of negatives by other photographers. The first is a series of village views by Dolby Bros of Stamford, many of which were used as postcards, and the second is a collection, lent by Stamford Museum, of photographs of a similar period from the Rutland Natural History & Archaeological Society. Few of the latter have ever been published.

The other principal source of photographs, well represented here, is the family album. All sorts of events, from the likely, such as the picnic tea party (page 40), to the unlikely, including butchering the family pig (page 86), were recorded for posterity. The subject matter can be anything, the quality may leave much to be desired, but without them our picture of the past would be much diminished.

The photographs have been arranged in several sections. Special attention is paid first to Oakham, the former county town, and still the principal market town of Rutland. It was never large, but its castle and county town status lent it a certain dignity and sense of place which it still maintains. Some of the earlier photographs record features, now gone, which today would be prized as being of historical or townscape value: the old shambles, the medieval jettied buildings of the Market Place, the lost wing of Flore's House, for example.

In the next section a whole range of special events and occasions and gatherings can be found, some public, some institutional, some more personal in nature. In many cases, the names of participants are recorded, but sometimes they are not. In some instances, no doubt, readers may be able to amplify the record and any such additional information will be gratefully received. The same applies to the third section, which concentrates on children and schooldays.

The countryman's way of life, represented next, has changed beyond recognition over the past century. Most of us live now at too fast a pace, and have lost that intimate contact, that weather eye, which forms an instinctive bond with nature and her ways. When we look at pictures of horses in harness at haytime or harvest, we see the contrast with the mechanized farm of today with a twinge of regret. Do we remember the hard work?

Although work on the land employed a far greater proportion of the population then than now, we should not forget the diversity of other work which people undertook for a living. In Rutland, quarrying for iron ore and building stone employed many people from the late nineteenth century until some twenty years ago. The specialist trades – blacksmith, wheelwright, tinsmith, cooper, to name but some – gave work for many more. Village communities were effectively self-sufficient for most of their simpler needs, as a glance at local trade directories will show, but they often relied on high street shops for more specialist goods and services. Some of these appear in the fifth section, followed by a look at forms of transport, whether horse and cart or train or motor vehicle, which have always captured the photographer's attention.

In the final section we indulge in a nostalgic ramble around the villages, in a roughly clockwise direction, with a selection of scenes which together typify the overall range of photographs which survive. Not every place in Rutland is illustrated. This is partly for reasons of space, but also partly because of deficiencies in some areas of the Rutland County Museum's collections. Indeed some of the larger places are under-represented.

If we look at these pictures with a view to identifying change, perhaps two examples are particularly noticeable. The first is the extent to which thatched roofs have dwindled in number, to be replaced either by Collyweston slates, or by more modern materials altogether – and not always sympathetically. Secondly, the early photographer could always find a motley collection of children, especially boys, with which to populate his pictures, whether or not they should have been at school!

If a book like this needs any dedication, it is not just to those photographers who made such an invaluable record of Rutland. It is also to all who have recognized the historical value and interest of this archive, preserved their photographs, annotated them with details of names and places, and have enabled them to be copied into the Rutland County Museum's records. Let us hope that others will follow their example.

T.H.McK.Clough
October 1993

SECTION ONE

Oakham: County Town

AERIAL VIEW OF OAKHAM

An aerial view of Oakham from the north-east. The castle and its earthworks can be seen in the foreground, with the church beyond. To the right is the original school building of 1584. This perspective emphasizes how crudely the extension of Church Street in the 1830s cut across the original rectangular Norman stronghold. Although there was some growth in the nineteenth century, it was only in the present century that the town began to expand significantly; many streets that we take for granted do not yet exist on this photograph, taken in the 1920s.

This fine early timber-framed building on the High Street frontage of the Market Place was replaced by a late Victorian stone building.

Thatched stone houses and shops on the corner of the High Street and Church Street which have also disappeared.

The Buttercross and Market Place, in one of the few views to show the covered market shambles, visible in the background, and thus before 1880. A poster on the Buttercross advertises a lecture by Mr J.S. Smith MA.

The Market Place in wartime, a sorry contrast with earlier views. A brick air raid shelter proclaims 'Lend to defend the right to be free'. On the right, boarded-up buildings await demolition.

The Market Place, 1913. This aspect attracted many photographers, with the pump on the left and, behind, a range of shops, including F.W. Hart's provision stores advertising home-cured hams and bacon of the highest quality. On the right is Perkins' general shop, with pairs of hobnail boots hanging on a rail outside.

The approach to Oakham Castle, 1916. Both sides of the lane from the Market Place were once lined with buildings of character. Those in this picture were demolished in 1950 to make way for a new post office, metropolitan in scale and concept. Its back yard is over the castle moat. The thirteenth-century gateway was rebuilt by George Villiers, Duke of Buckingham, in the early seventeenth century. Its wrought iron gates date from a further rebuilding in 1872, when the previous wooden ones, hung with horseshoes, were replaced.

A carriage with liveried attendants waits outside The Crown, a coaching inn in the High Street, in 1890. It was for the conveyance of a judge at the Rutland Assizes, which were held at the castle.

Oakham Castle and church. Seen from the south-east, the Great Hall of the Norman castle (right) is dwarfed by a great chestnut tree.

Photography in court is normally forbidden, but this record was made of the Rutland Assizes in 1947.

Lord Lane, Lord Chief Justice, presided over a Crown Court which was held during the 800th anniversary celebrations at Oakham Castle in 1981. He was presented with a posy on his arrival (above), and then paid a forfeit of a horseshoe to E.R. Hanbury, Lord of the Manor of Oakham, in accordance with age-old custom.

The Oakham Town Band plays solemnly and gentlemen doff their hats as the death of Queen Victoria is announced at Oakham Castle on a cold and foggy day in January 1901.

The late twelfth-century Great Hall of Oakham Castle. The church can be seen beyond the remains of the inner bailey wall. This photograph was taken in 1915 by Henton.

Oakham church from Cutts Close. This collotype view clearly shows the earthworks and remaining perimeter walls of Oakham Castle, degraded and overgrown, and, to the right, the original sixteenth-century Oakham School building.

The view down Catmose Street, including the Bell Inn, in 1967, before the demolition and realignment of the road, and the building of a new library by Rutland County Council.

The corner of High Street and Mill Street in 1969, shortly before the demolition of Smith's shop and the Oxfam centre.

The High Street, 1913. This bottleneck, once known as Bargate, was the town's earliest victim of traffic improvement schemes. On the left stands Flore's House, a late fourteenth-century house built by William Flore, one of Oakham's most successful self-made men. The end bay, then Fligge's boot and shoe shop, was taken down and the cross wing rebuilt the year after Henton took this photograph. On the right is the Red Lion, licensee David Bryan, selling J. Furley & Co.'s wines and spirits, itself later demolished.

Dean Street, running parallel to the High Street, was in the manor of Oakham Deanshold (belonging to the Abbey of Westminster), and was for long the most densely populated and poorest part of the town. Many households lived in close proximity, with shared primitive sanitation and communal pumps for water. In 1917, Henton made this unusual study of its inhabitants, all carefully posed for visual effect. The hand delivery cart of Melton Co-operative Society's No. 2 Branch is prominently placed in the centre.

Cold Overton Road, 'Oakham by the Sea', following severe rain in August 1922. 'We did not get flooded . . . not a spot thro' our roof, but plenty at No 8,' wrote the sender of this postcard.

Sawdust and greasepaint in Oakham as the circus comes to town in 1934 – an action photograph in the big top as the tightrope walker crosses the ring.

An auction in the Victoria Hall (formerly the Agricultural Hall) in the High Street, in 1934. The auctioneer was Ivan Atton.

All Saints' has a fine ring of eight bells. These were taken down for recasting in 1910. The standing bell bears the name of J. Taylor, the famous Loughborough bell foundry.

A topiary horse in the garden of Justus Littler, veterinary surgeon, off Station Road, as it was in the 1930s.

A collotype print of the rockery garden at Catmose, the home of the Oakham branch of the Noel family. The extensive gardens were planted with many specimen trees and shrubs.

John Thomas Riley (right) outside his drapers shop in the Market Place in about 1867, when he was 25. He had moved to Stamford by 1870.

SECTION TWO

Special Occasions

A traditional Boxing Day meet of the Cottesmore hounds, a familiar part of the countryman's yearly cycle, gets under way in Cutts Close. The close was part of the outer grounds of Oakham Castle, where in medieval times there were fish-ponds and gardens.

Sir Henry Tate Bt presents a cup outside
Constables, the former Uppingham
workhouse, at a horse show held in 1948.

The Cottesmore hounds meet in the quadrangle of Uppingham School, thirty years ago.
The gathering took place outside the hall built to commemorate old boys who died in
the First World War. The headmaster, Martin Lloyd (right, wearing gown), and boys
look on.

Judging shire mares at the Rutland Agricultural Society's annual show on the showground on the edge of Oakham, *c.* 1930. The society was founded in 1831 and the shows soon became a focal point of the local farming year. When the photograph was taken, the heavy horse was still very much an essential element of farming – note the waggons in the background.

At the Rutland Agricultural Show in the 1930s. Captain and Mrs Whadcoat, Miss Watson and Mrs Payton (above), and Mrs Carlos Clarke (Lady Eileen Clarke) and her children Diana and Sandy (below).

E3. Lord Lonsdale with
'Royal Lancer,' Winner
of the St Leger,
Doncaster, Sep. 1922

Hugh Lowther, 5th Earl of Lonsdale, was a larger-than-life figure, well known throughout Rutland and still remembered. In 1922, his horse 'Royal Lancer' won the St Leger at Doncaster, no doubt to the benefit of betting men in Rutland, though the sender of the postcard above says he wasn't so lucky. Below, Lord and Lady Lonsdale, with Lord Gretton (centre), at a presentation.

Ketton was renowned for its success in quoits competitions, and here one of the village teams proudly displays its trophies.

What a catch! 'A photo of the fish we caught on Boxing Day. The largest of them weighted [sic] 8¾ lbs,' wrote Bert, the sender of this postcard. The total weight of these pike, taken from Burley fish-ponds on 26 December 1905, was 78 lb.

Richard Westbrook Baker jun. (back right), of Langham, joined the Leicestershire Yeomanry, and served in the Boer War. He was photographed in Winburg, South Africa, by Heinrich Franz.

Leicestershire Imperial Yeomanry on parade in Oakham during their annual camp in 1908, shortly before full 'territorialization'. Many Rutland men volunteered to serve in the regiment.

The Rutland Volunteer Regiment. The volunteers paraded at Oakham with their motor cars and motorcycles for inspection by Field Marshall Lord French of Ypres on 13 May 1917, the anniversary of the battle of Frezenberg in 1915 in which many Leicestershire Yeomanry men had died.

CQMS Alfred Steward, of B Company, 1st Battalion Rutland Volunteer Regiment, came from Uppingham, where he was in business as a hairdresser, known locally as Sweeney Todd.

A unique flintlock light field gun by William Embrey of Wing, seemingly made for local defence use in about 1795. It bears the arms of the Earl of Gainsborough and was once at Exton Park. It was sold at Sotheby's in 1968, and its whereabouts are now unknown.

Uppingham Auxiliary Hospital. Built as the workhouse for the Uppingham Union, in the First World War it served as a hospital. Now it is a boarding house for Uppingham School.

During the Second World War, Burley on the Hill, like many other country houses, served as a convalescent hospital. Patricia Baxter (above) was a VAD nurse here in 1940 to 1941. Below, her fellow nurses and their patients, in hospital blue with red ties, gather on the steps.

Music in the Market Place. There is clearly a festive air as crowds mingle with the Town Band in Oakham in August 1907. The message on the back of this postcard reads: 'Can you find Jim and Winnie on this . . . I was not there or it would not have been so good.'

Past and present officers of the Rutland Lodge of the Manchester Unity of Oddfellows outside the east end of Oakham Castle, before the mullioned window was blocked up. The photograph was taken by H.P. Holt of Oakham in 1910.

The Leicestershire Yeomanry take part in a festive parade along Oakham High Street.

Two members of the Leicestershire Yeomanry in full dress uniform at Oakham Castle.

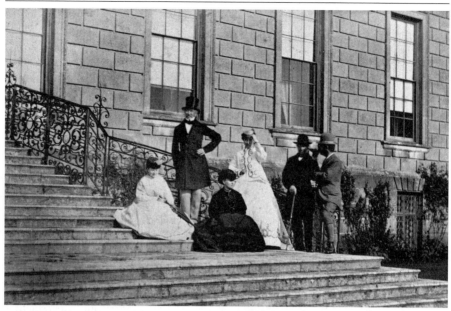

Members of the Finch family pose on the steps of their mansion at Burley on the Hill.

Lady Fludyer, from Ayston Hall, and guests take a picnic tea in the fields at Wardley.

A carefully arranged family portrait at Ketton.

Tea in the garden for the Morris family on a fine afternoon in Barrowden. Tables and chairs, cloths and cake stands, and the best china have been brought out for the occasion.

A Church Army missionary van in Whissendine in 1904, with its three accompanying preachers.

The Revd John Clifford. One of a long series of visiting preachers, Dr Clifford came to Oakham on 8 February 1905. His likeness was sent on a postcard to Mr Morris, bookdealer, of Barrowden.

The Bishop of Peterborough at Ketton for the dedication of the new vestry in 1935, with Brigadier General R. St G. Gorton, Vicar's Warden, and C.F. Burroughes, People's Warden.

The funeral procession of the Earl of Gainsborough draws past Exton Hall, the coffin in a farm wagon piled high with flowers. A policeman stands discreetly against the front of the house.

Where Uppingham had Paul David and nearby Stamford had Malcolm Sargent, Oakham boasted Henry Nicholson ARCO, music teacher at the school, church organist and choirmaster. The photograph was taken outside the summerhouse of Flore's House, his home until he died in November 1922.

Oakham Ladies' Choir at Burley on the Hill. Back row: Miss Hilda Pettifer, Miss Ethel Ball, Miss M. Alderwood, Miss D. Healey, Miss E. Grinter. Front row: Miss K. Franks, -?- , Mr H. Nicholson, Miss V. Wearn, Mrs Axtell Gardiner.

Celebrations at North Luffenham. This postcard photograph was sent with the following message: 'Dear Flo, This is the little crowd that had the Wedding Breakfast. You will know a few of them. With love, Pattie.'

A wedding group assembles outside Nos 12 and 14 Church Street, Braunston.

Ketton people taking part in a theatrical performance gather at Northwick Hall, Ketton, in 1910.

Villagers in their finery pose for the photographer by the pond at Barrowden, with the Exeter Arms in the background.

Part of a great carnival parade in Oakham, with Mrs Anne Haywood, the wife of Rutland's Lord Lieutenant, in the role of Elizabeth I.

Members of the Ridlington & Preston Women's Institute take part in a revue, 'Vintage '65', in Preston Village Hall during the WI diamond jubilee year.

'Votes for Women!', cry the suffragettes outside the Angel Inn, Northgate, Oakham. If you look carefully, however, you will find that they are all men!

Villagers gather for the annual Ketton Feast, always held on the first Sunday after 15 August.

Olave, Lady Baden-Powell GBE, World Chief Guide, greets a member of the 1st Oakham Guides on her visit to Oakham Castle on 17 April 1966.

Sir Kenneth Ruddle takes the salute as the Guides march past in the St George's Day parade in Oakham in 1964, recorded by the *Stamford Mercury*.

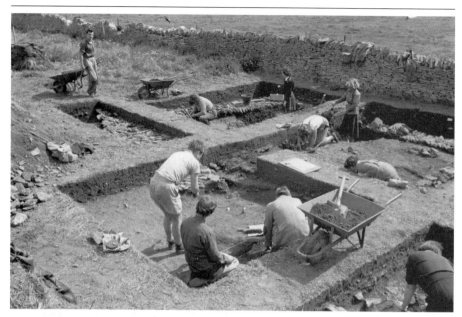

Great Casterton was the site of a Roman town, with adjacent to it a fort and a villa. These were the subject of excavations in summer schools, arranged by the University of Nottingham, in the 1950s and '60s. Here, in 1956, a Roman building is excavated.

The Great Casterton excavation team, led by Dr Philip Corder, outside the secondary school which formed their base, in 1958.

Box trenches in line, recalling Mortimer Wheeler's military-style approach to archaeological excavation, along the eastern boundary wall of Sharpe's farm, Great Casterton, 1956.

The inaugural meeting of the Friends of the Rutland County Museum at Casterton in 1959, with (left to right) A.H. Capendale, E.G. Bolton, B. Ellis, D. Davenport-Handley, Mrs A. Ellis, and Sir K. Ruddle.

Sir Kenneth Ruddle (left), Chairman of the Rutland County Council, and Alan Bond, Clerk to the Council, proudly displaying the gold cufflinks with which they were presented in 1963 after the successful fight to retain the county's independence.

SECTION THREE

Schooldays and Playtime

Boys and girls at Casterton drawing a Davey Sleep balance plough (now in the Rutland County Museum) in an art class. Note the contemporary sculpture in the background. The school was opened in 1939, and gathered its pupils from the rural communities of eastern Rutland. Later, it became a secondary modern school and is now a community college.

Writing an essay about 'The Invisible Man', at Casterton when the school opened in 1939.

Schoolboys with hoes? This was typical of the headmaster E.G. Bolton's pragmatic approach to education at Casterton, where children from rural backgrounds gained practical experience as well as academic knowledge.

Not a ritual dance, but headmaster and pupils sharing the chore of picking stones from the school's future sports field at Casterton in 1939.

A sports day display at Casterton Secondary Modern School.

The pupils and teacher of the village school at Ketton, *c.* 1921.

The village National School at Langham, around the turn of the century.

Christine Straw receives her present from Father Christmas at Langham School, as fellow pupils look on.

Young ladies at the 'Institution de Mme Charity' in Mill Street, Oakham, carefully assembled with their croquet gear. They don't look very happy!

The Rutland Musical Competitions used to attract entries from across the county. In 1907, the Bisbrooke and Glaston School singing class won a prize.

School Lane, Uppingham, before the building of the Memorial Hall and the Freemasons' Gates. Meadows the bootmaker has premises on the right, beyond the old studies.

The Fludyers' carriage, from Ayston, takes part in an official visit to Uppingham School.

The school tower in Uppingham, opposite the abattoir. Even the youthful compiler remembers Friday Greek lessons in its classroom (no doubt studying Homer's *Odyssey*) to the accompaniment of squealing pigs, and the smell of burnt cabbage from the school porter's rooms below.

The old hall and quadrangle at Uppingham School, with some of the boys' old studies. The school was one of the first public schools to provide individual study rooms for its pupils.

The wartime National Egg Collection. Barrowden collectors, including a Boy Scout and a Girl Guide, proudly announce their grand total of 12,000 eggs.

The infants of Oakham Primary School pose for their annual photograph in 1908. Behind them is a mud wall, a rare sight nowadays.

The Second World War seems far away in this tranquil scene on the Chater, but in fact the boy is an evacuee who stayed with Pat Walpole at Ketton.

The crowning of the May Queen was one of the high points of the country year, celebrated in many Rutland villages. Here, the North Luffenham May Queen is surrounded by her fellow pupils at the village primary school.

The May Queen and her attendants at Braunston.

The May Queen at Cottesmore, with the garlanded canopy which was carried with her in the festival procession.

Choosing the May Queen at Cottesmore. Notice the swing-boats behind the trees on the right, and the parade of Boy Scouts, complete with staffs, in the background on the left.

The May Queen, North Luffenham, 1916. The village primary school kept an album of postcards, including one of this garlanded maiden.

SECTION FOUR

Life in the Country

Uppingham Market Place, *c.* 1900. Farmers' tongues wag outside Coltman's the ironmongers.

Ben Painter, of Cow Close Farm, Burley, was a very well known figure in Rutland, famous for his Lincoln and Leicester longwool sheep, and secretary of the Rutland Agricultural Society for sixteen years, retiring in 1893. He died in 1915.

Sheep in Oakham Market Place, once a regular sight. On the right is the George Hotel, one of the town's two coaching inns. Furley & Hassan occupy part of the central block, built in 1890. The cattle market continues today on a site off South Street.

A sheep market in Uppingham Market Place.

Crowds at the regular sheep and cattle market at Uppingham. This market was already well established when the Oakham cattle market was set up in 1830, but gradually lost ground until now only the traditional Christmas fatstock market is held.

Wool was naturally a staple commodity and many sheep were raised in Rutland. Shearing was done by hand in the early summer and was a scene of great activity, as at Lyddington (above) and Barrowden (below).

Mr Burton, once a shepherd for Bradshaws'
at Egleton, retired to Simper Street,
Oakham. He knitted socks in the First
World War, and is shown wearing the medal
of Queen Mary's Needlework Guild.

Sheep watering at Barrowden village pond. The pond was not only a watering and
washing place for animals, but was also used to swell the wooden wheels of farm
waggons when they dried out in hot weather.

'Oakham Dainty', one of the champion milking cows from the Catmose Park Farm, Oakham.

A prize bull, one of several such photographs taken near the medieval motte-and-bailey castle of Alstoe, near Burley.

Members of the Rutland Young Farmers Club pose for a photograph at Oakham cattle market, South Street, *c.* 1930.

A placid scene in Braunston in 1930. Dairy cows amble gently up the village street. In the background Mr Rawlings the postman stops for a chat with Mrs Buxton.

A farm in the hamlet of Pilton in 1916. The square stone dovecote is typical of many in the Rutland area.

A farmyard scene at Wing in 1915, hinting at the simplicity, and perhaps poverty, of rural life. What does the old man with his milk can peering from the doorway think of the photographer?

The gamekeeper's daughter, Gwen Masters. The badger was found in Burley Wood, and Gwen kept it as a pet in their cottage on the Stamford Road.

A welcome break for members of the Morley family in the harvest field at Teigh.

Jack Robinson, with 'Bonnie', takes the wooden haysweep up the hillside at Hambleton. In the background can be seen Burley Woods.

Landscape study by Henton of Nether Hambleton, July 1913. The village was badly affected by the Black Death in the fourteenth century. The remains of deserted properties survived in nearby fields until flooded beneath Rutland Water.

Mr A.E. Wild in the hayfield, with the horse rake, at Hambleton.

A good job done, as the workers on the Morleys' farm at Teigh pose with a laden wagon.

Looking across the valley from the neatly stooked harvest fields of Ketton towards the spot where two Dakotas from Spanhoe airfield, Northamptonshire, collided and crashed on 8 July 1944, killing all but one of the American and Polish troops on board. The survivor, Corporal T. Chambers, was saved because he landed in soft river mud.

Haymaking at Hambleton, on the Wilds' farm. Just visible in the background is a stationary engine driving the hay elevator.

Edward Ball's farmhands pose in front of his lorry and a nearly complete stack in the farmyard in Burley Road, Oakham. Seated on the ground in front is Fred Laxton.

A 1910 Allchin traction engine, made in Northampton, with a road train of loaded harvest wagons at Langham.

The sale of a white horse at stables in Northgate Street, Oakham, near the printing works of Thomas Walker.

Mr W. Lawrence of Preston and his Ruston & Hornsby steam engine in 1965.

Prolific hives reach ambitiously upwards in the flower garden at Barrowden where
Edward Morris produced his honey.

Capturing the bees. Two experienced beekeepers at Barrowden unconcernedly pose by their straw skep as they gather the swarm.

Inspecting the combs. This time suitably protected, the apiarist looks to see if all is well in the hive and checks the completeness of the honeycombs.

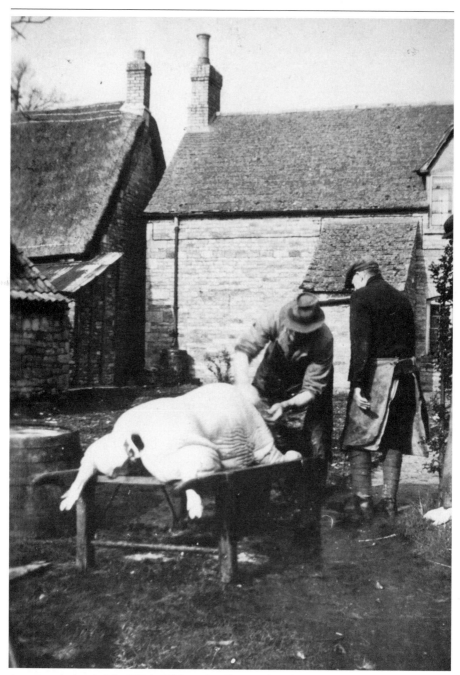

An annual ritual. Mr Elijah Tibbert butchers a family pig at Edith Weston. Many families kept a pig to provide meat, hams and bacon for the winter; after all, you could use it all except the squeal.

SECTION FIVE

Earning a Living

Ketton quarrymen. The oolitic limestone of the Ketton pits, occurring as a freestone, was transported far and wide. Much went to Cambridge for use in college buildings. The history of exploitation is a long one and indeed some building stone is still produced. However, the traditional methods used by men such as these are now a thing of the past and the main product, on an increasing scale, is Portland cement.

The Ketco cement works at Ketton, with a sail-reaper and Fordson tractor at work in the foreground.

A stone quarry, probably at Clipsham.

Two views of the ironstone quarries at Market Overton. Above, workmen with full wooden wheelbarrows move the overburden across planks on tall trestles so that it can be used to restore the land already quarried. A long jib shovel works in the background. Below, the working face is undercut and the ore is loaded into waiting trucks.

Moving an excavator across the Thistleton to Sewstern road – a cooperative venture also involving Post Office telephone engineers and the local farmer's straw.

The first electric 'navvy', made by Ruston Bucyrus, arrives on E.W. Rudd's heavy transporter at Market Overton quarries in 1930.

A rake of wooden side-tipper waggons in the ironstone quarries at Burley. Very few of these waggons now survive, but they were a commonplace sight in the quarries.

Luffenham flour mills, on the railway at South Luffenham, opened in 1892, only to close thirty years later as a victim of the depression. Waggons of the South Normanton Colliery Company and the Midland Railway stand in the sidings.

Seaton mills, July 1913. A Domesday Book reference suggests that there had probably been a watermill here on the Welland since at least the eleventh century. The wooden post-mill overlooking it, evidently moved here only in 1881, was dismantled a few years after this view was photographed. The railway viaduct, built between 1876 and 1878, with its eighty-two arches, forms a backdrop to one of Henton's most successful and striking landscape compositions.

The post-mill at Preston, documented in the early nineteenth century and demolished in 1926, stood near the Ridlington road in a position guaranteed to catch the wind.

Bland & Son's house at Greetham. Involvement in church restoration work enabled the firm to incorporate substantial architectural fragments in the walls.

Thatchers at work, replacing the roof on a cottage in Exton. The master thatcher was W.H. Halliday, who worked for the Earl of Gainsborough's estate for many years.

Wheelwrights tyring a wheel at Whissendine, *c.* 1940. The hot iron tyre is dropped over the assembled wheel. Here, Jack Dobney, wheelwright (back left), and W. Wigginton, blacksmith (front right), H. Hall and R. Exton cool the tyre with water so that it shrinks and tightens all the joints.

A.E. Ward of Egleton, wheelwright, and his men with a new dray for Ellis & Everard's Oakham depot. Some of his tools are now in the Rutland County Museum.

The smithy at Burley on the Hill. What could be more evocative of rural England than this chocolate-box image of a horse being shod 'under a spreading chestnut tree'. Indeed, the Burley smithy is claimed to be the inspiration for Longfellow's famous poem about the blacksmith.

Fountain's woodyard at Greetham. Most of Henton's photographs are of village street scenes, houses and churches, but occasionally he made a study like this of a working environment. This one is full of interest, from the men with the timber drug and the loaded wagon beyond, to the shrouded steam traction engine on the right. All around is the seemingly casual clutter of everyday working life, but in it the human figures and the horses have been carefully placed to enhance the composition.

The post office at Whissendine, *c.* 1906. On the right stands James Gamble, the postman, with his bicycle and parcel cart. The telegraph boy on the left is possibly Harold Stringer.

Oakham Post Office staff in a formal group outside the office in the High Street, photographed by A.E. Billows of Oakham.

Frederick Sharpe's advertisement. On the corner of High Street and Church Street, Oakham, Sharpe's ironmongery, founded in the mid-nineteenth century, was a major emporium.

High Street, Uppingham, 1916. On the left is The Crown, an RAC listed hotel. On the right, beyond the hairdresser's sign, the front of the glass and china shop (advertising Goss China) boasts exterior gas lights.

Mrs Mary Ann Nichols ran a hardware
business, Nichols & Son, in Uppingham
from around 1907. Above is shown their
travelling dray with Walter, her youngest
son, driving. It is loaded with goods for sale,
mostly kitchen utensils, ready for a trip
around the villages. Below, Mrs Nichols in
her Bath chair, beside the London Road.

D.E. Clarke's shop, 33 High Street, Oakham. In the window are dog foods by Entwistle's of Liverpool, Liverine (for fish), and Capern's bird seed. Mr Clarke was also licensed to sell tobacco.

International Stores, 24 High Street, Oakham. The photograph was taken in 1922 or 1923, when Jackson & Boston, ironmongers, were to the left and Stevens' ladies' department was to the right. Salmon was on promotion, and margarine was 10d a pound.

E.D. Smith's tobacconists shop in the Market Place, Oakham, demolished in 1950. He stocked 'Cottesmore' cigarettes and ran a circulating library.

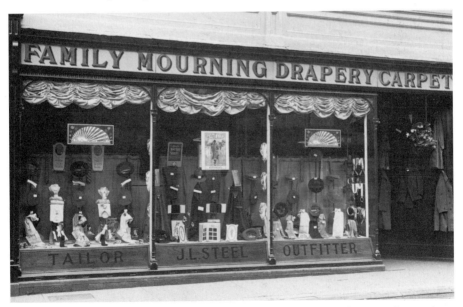

J.L. Steel's shop on the corner of High Street and Mill Street, Oakham. In the windows are displayed the new season's goods, including navy blue serges and 'Peltinvain' weathercoats.

The straight-railed waggon belonging to Molesworth's brewery, outside the Aveland Arms in Bull Lane, Ketton, where the licensee was William Cliff.

Furley & Hassan's smart covered removal waggons at the corner of High Street and Burley Road, Oakham. Many years later, the remains of one of these were found in a fenland yard.

The White Horse at Empingham, while John Pretty was landlord between 1916 and 1926.

The Blue Ball at Manton in around 1925, with Mrs Mary Myers (left), the licensee from 1910 to 1935, and her daughter Mrs Baines. This was a Northampton Brewery Company house.

Benjamin and Lilian Walker and their father set out on the milk round from Langham to Oakham.

Delivering the milk, on the corner of William Dalby Street, Oakham. Charlie Grimmer and Mrs Dexter stand in the doorway; the latter let rooms to hunting people in the season.

J. Gunn of Barrowden, shoemaker, who died in October 1896 aged 91, a stalwart of a village trade now lost. Some of his tools are in the Rutland County Museum.

W.H. Smith & Son's bookstall on the southbound platform at Oakham station, complete with staff and delivery boys. Nottingham to St Pancras trains called here, and there was always a demand for newspapers and other reading matter for the journey.

The last days of the letterpress and typesetting by hand at Matkins' printing works, off Oakham High Street. Matkins was the most prolific of the town's printers, and until 1941 produced annual almanacks covering the Oakham postal district.

SECTION SIX

Transport

The Railway Hotel, Essendine. This eastern Rutland village lies on the main London to Scotland line, and once provided a minor branch link to Stamford.

The station at Manton junction, whence one could take a train direct to London St Pancras. In the forecourt is 'Tiny' Thorpe with his Uppingham to Manton conveyance.

The station at Uppingham, at the head of the short, steep branch line from Seaton junction. At the end of term, boys from the school would walk from their boarding houses with their cases early in the morning to catch a special train.

Ketton level crossing in the 1930s. A Midland Railway notice to the right advertises the 'passenger's luggage in advance' service for 1s or 6d. Today, only the signal box survives.

Seaton junction, with a
single carriage connection
for the Uppingham
branch waiting at the
platform.

Miss Gwendoline Finch with her donkey cart at Oakham station.

Luffenham station, and a lift home in FP 3378. This was wartime: note the white-painted bumper and the mask on the nearside light (the offside light went out when the driver dipped the headlights).

Luffenham station closed in 1966 like so many other rural stations. The main buildings and the sidings were removed soon afterwards.

A bridge and watersplash at South Luffenham, a verdant summer scene taken by Henton in July 1913.

Bridge over the Gwash, Empingham. On the busy road to Stamford, this was the scene of an ambitious widening scheme by Rutland County Council in 1958, which retained the bridge parapets in new positions.

The Ayston crossroads. Photographed perhaps a century ago, the view shows the village nestling among the trees, the church just visible in the background.

The bridge at Caldecott with the adjacent mill. This is Rutland's southernmost village, and faces across the flood plain of the Welland towards Rockingham and its castle.

Low-slung transport at Braunston.

Crowds look on as a coach and four take part in the grand parade at the Rutland Agricultural Show, held in Oakham every August until recently.

The horse-drawn Oakham fire engine on the corner of South Street and Mill Street.

A.E. Wild with his waggon and two heavy horses, smartly turned out for judging at the Rutland Agricultural Show.

A dreamy summer view down Brooke Hill towards Oakham, July 1914.

The church and Church Lane, South Luffenham, in 1916, a view which has since changed little, although the foot-bridge and its railings have been renewed.

Digging out the snowdrifts on Empingham Hill, Ketton, during the prolonged winter freeze of early 1947.

Floods by Braunston churchyard. Modern water management has greatly reduced the incidence and impact of flooding, but even in the 1960s the stream here could rise by nearly 10 feet.

In June 1916, J.E. Baines of Mill Street, Oakham, supplied a new 25 hp 30½ cwt Whiting Demby truck, FP 671, to the Belvoir Vale Dairies, Harby. Here it is outside the garage.

T.C. Molesworth's Regal 6 hp four-seater, FP 62, which was first registered under the new legal requirements of January 1904, shown here in later years.

John Norton of Braunston, riding his 1920 Zenith 350 cc motorcycle.

At the Rutland Agricultural Show, Charlie Lenton drives FP 4, a 1898 8 hp Decauville which belonged to George Phillips, Inspector of Weights and Measures for Rutland and local historian. The car is still in running order.

Propaganda on the Great North Road! Rutland's twin slogans of 'Rutland fights to keep local government local' and 'Rutland fights for minority rights' assailed the public and government alike in its second successful fight to retain county status in 1962/3.

A new surface dressing for Burley Road, Oakham, in 1934.

Around the Villages

The gatehouse at Brooke Priory, built in conjunction with its ornamental gardens, is all that survives of a great house built here by the Noel family, Earls of Gainsborough, after the dissolution of the small Augustinian priory, Rutland's only full monastery. The present house probably incorporates parts of the priory, and indeed a fine early thirteenth-century reliquary with Limoges enamel decoration was found here in 1805. The photograph was taken by Henton in July 1914.

St Peter's, Brooke, one of Rutland's most special churches. Much of the work is Elizabethan, with remodelled sixteenth- and seventeenth-century pews and fittings inside.

Cottages at Brooke. Once picturesque, they have now lost their thatch, and have long since been sadly mutilated by inappropriate dormer windows, asbestos tiles and corrugated iron.

A gathering on Braunston village green, evidently for the auction of a horse belonging to Mr Bickby, a Methodist preacher, who refused to pay a levy due under the Education Act of 1902.

Main Street, Braunston, now a busy thoroughfare. The upper end of the street is flanked by substantial ironstone houses, the nearest one with a date stone of 1660.

The approach to Ashwell church, 1913. In the 1850s, Viscount Downe commissioned William Butterfield's restoration of the church as well as cottages and estate buildings in the village.

The hamlet of Barleythorpe, just to the north of Oakham, the site of Lord Lonsdale's Rutland home and of the famous Barleythorpe stud.

Well Street, Langham, with a village pump on the left. The cottages on the right are no longer there.

The Manor House, Langham, a substantial seventeenth-century house, as seen by Henton in August 1913.

St Peter and St Paul's, Langham, with the floor traditionally strewn with hay from a field given to the church, for the Langham Feast on the first Sunday after 29 June.

Harvest thanksgiving at Brooke, and the church is appropriately decorated.

Burley on the Hill, formerly the seat of the Earls of Winchelsea and Nottingham. The gardens were remodelled by Humphrey Repton at the end of the eighteenth century. He created this deep terrace on the southern aspect, which now overlooks Rutland Water.

An excellent view of the hermitage, a folly in the grounds of Burley on the Hill, by Cooke, the Hambleton schoolmaster. Charles G. & S. Cooke advertised in *Matkin's Almanack* of 1904 as photographic artists.

The former entrance lodge at Barnsdale Hall, which now overlooks the north shore of Rutland Water.

St Edmund's church, Egleton, which boasts a good early doorway and chancel arch, was muffled in ivy when Henton visited it in September 1915, but it is not so now.

The Old Priest House at Hambleton, just below the hilltop church. Its roof is now tiled and the front wall supported by stone buttresses. At the time of Domesday Book in 1086, Hambleton was the centre of a royal estate which boasted three churches and three priests.

An unfriendly warning to beggars in the 'town' of Barrow recalls the days when passing vagrants were a common sight.

The hamlet of Barrow, overlooking the vale of Catmose, once had its own chapel. The remains of the village cross stand beside a derelict cottage, later restored.

Cottesmore Hall, which was seriously damaged by fire in 1926, was reconstructed, only to be demolished in 1974 after years standing empty.

Thatched limestone cottages at The Leas, Cottesmore, 1916. The lane was once known as Hack's Lane, after a well known local farming family.

The sheep dyke at Cottesmore, with cottages beyond. The pond was filled in forty years ago.

Cottesmore's spacious main street, with the church beyond and the village green to the right, photographed by Henton in April 1914.

A picturesque range of thatched cottages in High Street, Exton, which looks much the same today. The village postman stands with his bicycle in the shadows on the left of the picture.

The ruins of Exton Old Hall, a fine early seventeenth-century mansion which was gutted by fire in 1810. It was the main Rutland seat of the Noel family.

The horse pond at Exton, now filled in, was beside the road from Oakham, and was fed by a stream which ran through it. It was overlooked by the backs of cottages on the edge of the village.

A general view from Great Lane of the limestone village of Greetham, with pantiled cottages, now demolished, in the background.

The main street at Greetham, looking east, with the Black Horse on the left. The registration number of the approaching motor car is CT 896.

The Great North Road at Great Casterton. On the right is the Crown Inn, licensee J. Knight, where the poet John Clare had his wedding breakfast, and the cottage beyond is evidently in the process of being re-thatched.

Clipsham Rectory, notable for its unusual low-pitched main roof.

A cottage at Pickworth in 1905, next to the lime-kiln where John Clare worked for a while. Mrs John Clark stands on the left, with Tom in the middle and Aunt Eliza on the right.

Cottages at Geeston, an outlying hamlet of Ketton, 1916. The nearest house has now gone. The second, once thatched, has a date stone of 1670.

Church Street, Ketton, 1916. Little has altered in this view, except that the Railway Inn, on the left, is no longer thatched but has a Collyweston slate roof. The church, with its well known tower and spire, is a splendid example of thirteenth- and fourteenth-century ecclesiastical architecture, and one of Rutland's most ambitious churches.

The magnificent church of St Mary's, Ketton, seen from beyond the garden of The Priory, a former prebendal manor-house and one of the village's several substantial houses.

A typical limestone farmhouse in Ketton, roofed with Collyweston slates from the mines across the valley to the south.

The residents of St Mary's Diocesan Home, Ketton, many with babes in arms, are entertained at The Cottage, *c.* 1905. The home was set up in 1893 as 'a penitentiary for reforming young women' and training them for domestic service.

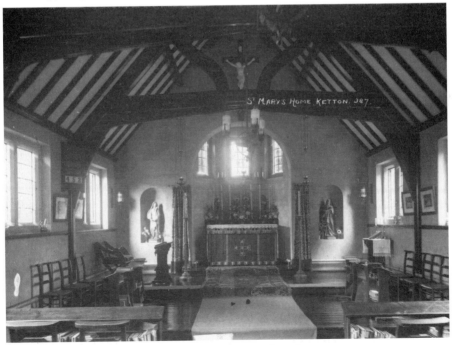

The chapel of St Mary's Home, now in use as a meeting place.

The Welland at Barrowden, 1916. The river, with its flourishing reed beds, forms the southern boundary of Rutland, separating it from Northamptonshire.

The Pattisson golf course tractor bought by Luffenham Heath Golf Club in 1938, with C. and D.J. Todd and others in winter snow. The tractor, which has a Ford engine, is now in the Rutland County Museum.

Single-storey outbuildings at Hall Farm, North Luffenham, 1916. Only their distant part now survives, but it has been well restored.

Cottage and garden study at South Luffenham. Taken in 1922, two years before he died, this is one of the last of Henton's Rutland photographs.

The exterior of Normanton church, showing the nave and chancel built by S.P. Cockerell in 1764 and demolished in 1911. The tower dates from the 1820s.

Coffins in the Heathcote family vault at Normanton before the rebuilding of the church.

The splendid mid-eighteenth century interior of Normanton church before the 1911 rebuilding, with memorials to members of the Heathcote family and, at the back, a tablet to the Venerable T.K. Bonney (Rector 1814–63, and Archdeacon of Leicester).

A study by Henton of the old parsonage at Edith Weston, taken in September 1916. The house, with its typical stone mullioned windows, dates at least in part from 1626. It stands sheltered by high walls next to the church. The village takes its name from Edith, the widow of Edward the Confessor, who held part of Rutland as her dowry in the eleventh century.

The floral bounty of old fashioned roses in a cottage garden at Edith Weston, captured by Henton in 1916.

Well Cross, Edith Weston, May 1916. Henton's pictures are always so carefully composed that it is something of a surprise to see his equipment case in the foreground!

A splendid mullion-windowed house, embellished with a two-storey bay window, overlooking the village green and the stocks at Market Overton, September 1913.

Cottages in Crocket Lane, Empingham, a byway which was once the scene of activity, with a busy wheelwright's premises.

A charming study of Lyndon church, clad in ivy and with climbing roses around the porch, taken by Henton in 1915. The climbers have all since been removed.

A Henton photograph of cottages in Post Office Lane, Lyndon. The motorcycle and side-car, FP 35, was a 2¼ hp de Dion, which belonged to the Oakham photographer Henry Ellingworth; did he go with Henton that day?

The last inhabited building at Martinsthorpe, now deserted, where the Earls of Denbigh once had a mansion.

A substantial seventeenth-century farm at Wing, in Main Street, opposite the church.

Newly thatched cottages on a steep lane in Bisbrooke, one of Rutland's smaller and more out of the way villages. This view is little changed today.

Caldecott is mostly an ironstone village, but several of its houses are strikingly built of alternating bands of limestone and ironstone. This one was disastrously rebuilt in 1951.

Belton Old Hall. A fine early seventeenth-century stone house, recorded by Henton one summer's day when the garden chairs were out.

Godfrey's House, Belton, 1914. This substantial mid-seventeenth century house, evidently once thatched, must have survived the terrible fire of 29 May 1776 which destroyed many cottages in the village.

St Peter's, Belton, before the building of a lich-gate in 1911. Much of the church dates from the thirteenth century, though the tower is a century or more later.

The Bishop of Lincoln's palace at Lyddington in 1913. Rutland was in the medieval diocese of Lincoln, and the bishop had a park here at least from the early thirteenth century until 1547. The mainly fifteenth-century palace was converted into a bedehouse for old people in the early seventeenth century, and continued as such until the late 1930s.

One of the last elderly residents of the bedehouse.

Houses on the green, Lyddington. Not only have all the thatch and creepers now gone, but so too has the gable end above the first-floor window, and the front wall of the house has been completely rebuilt since Henton took this photograph.

The manor-house at Wardley, with the churchyard on the left.

Though overall impressions remain the same, the changes in Ridlington's main street since 1915 when Henton took this photograph typify what has happened on the rural scene over the intervening years.

The snow-covered osier bed at Ketton, one of the last remnants of a rural industry which has now virtually disappeared.

Acknowledgements

Most of the photographs included in this book have been selected from the holdings of the Rutland County Museums, and the principal acknowledgement is to the Leicestershire Museums, Arts and Records Service for permission to use this invaluable archive. Also within this service is the Leicestershire Record Office, which has permitted me to use many photographs from the Henton Collection, and has provided reference copies for local use. Special thanks are due to Catherine Lines and her former colleague Steve Thursfield for undertaking so much photographic work in connection with both the Rutland County Museum's collection and this compilation.

Lincolnshire County Council (Recreational Services, Heritage Division, Stamford Museum) has kindly given permission to use a number of photographs from the Rutland Natural History and Archaeological Society's former collection now deposited at the Rutland County Museum.

The photographic archive built up over the years at the museum consists of original photographs given or lent to the collections and of copy photographs made from originals lent for reference. The Rutland Local History (and Record) Society has been instrumental here. A list follows of those whose photographs have been selected for inclusion, and without whose help and cooperation such an archive could not have been compiled. Grateful thanks are offered to all of them, and apologies are tendered if any should inadvertently have been omitted.

A.W. Arnold • J. Ball • Miss T. Bamford • Mrs W.M. Beardshall
Mrs E.D. Beeson • Mrs G.E. Broadhurst • Mr and Mrs A.H. Capendale
Casterton Community College • A.D. Clark • Mrs A.E. Dalby • Mrs E. Dickson
Dolby Bros of Stamford • Mrs P.M. Edmunds • Major J.M. Ellingworth
G.H. Finch • F. Frith & Co. Ltd • Miss M. Gibson • C. Green • G. Green
R.F. Grimwood • H.E. Gunn • Dr D.P. Harris • J. Hassan • Mrs C.M. Isaac
Langham WI • J.F. Levisohn ARPS • Mr Lickman • Mrs Marriott
Matkins Printers Ltd • K. Meadwell • G.R. Morley • W.R.F. Munton
Mrs V.M. Noel-Paton • NE Scotland Library Service
North Luffenham C. of E. Primary School
Northampton & County Independent • Mrs J. Norton • E.W. Palmer • J. Palmer
Ridlington & Preston WI • Rutland District Council
Rutland Railway Museum • Mrs Ryder • J. Southerill • Mrs Stafford Smith
Stamford Mercury • Mrs M. Steele • J. Steward • Miss D.V. Stimson • Mrs Stubbs
D.H. Tew • Miss L. Walker • Mrs J. Wild • Mrs Winter • Miss E.L. Woodward